it's time to
color,
unwind, and
relax!

Pour yourself a glass of wine,

coffee, or tea and let's get

started!

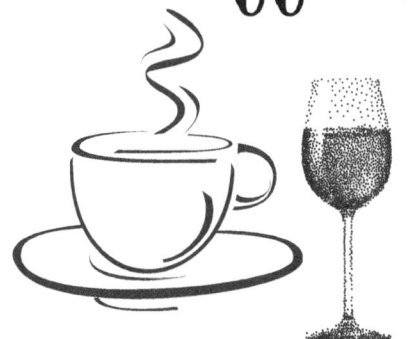

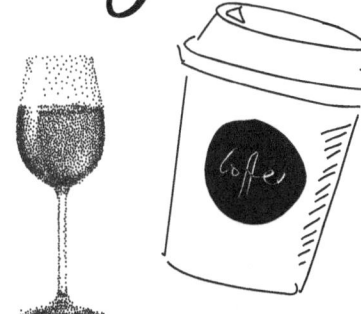

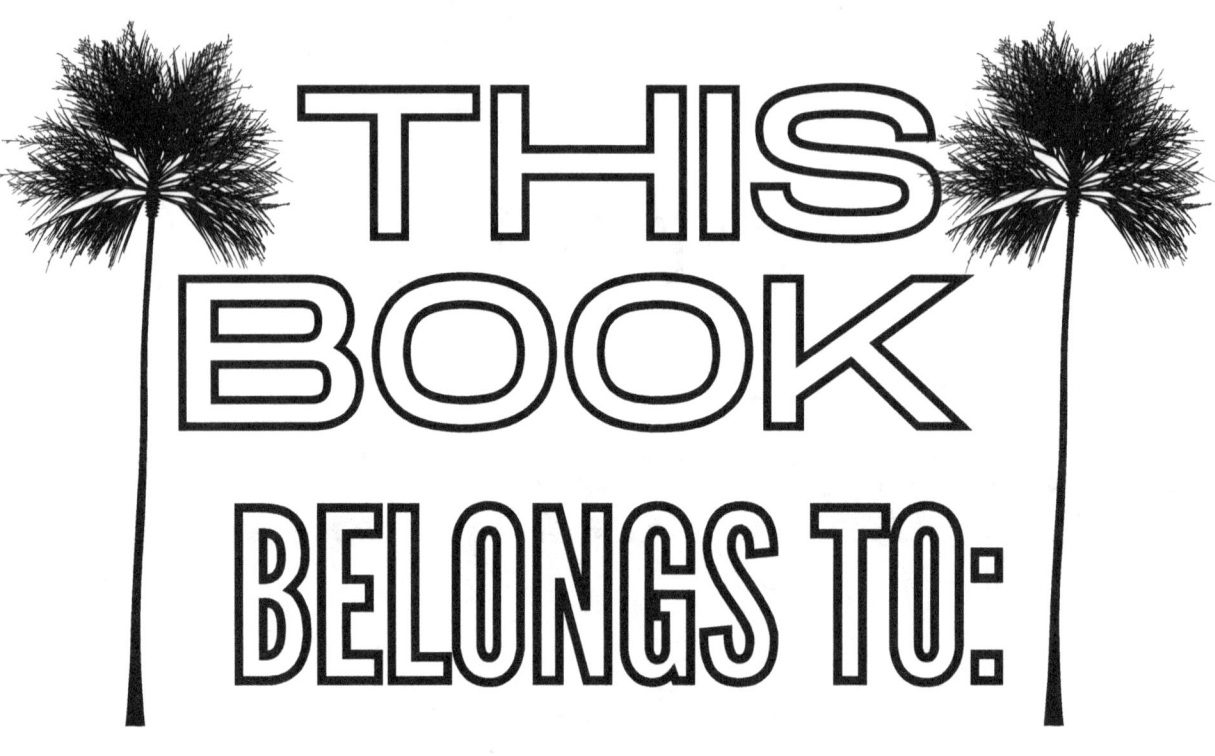

THIS BOOK

BELONGS TO:

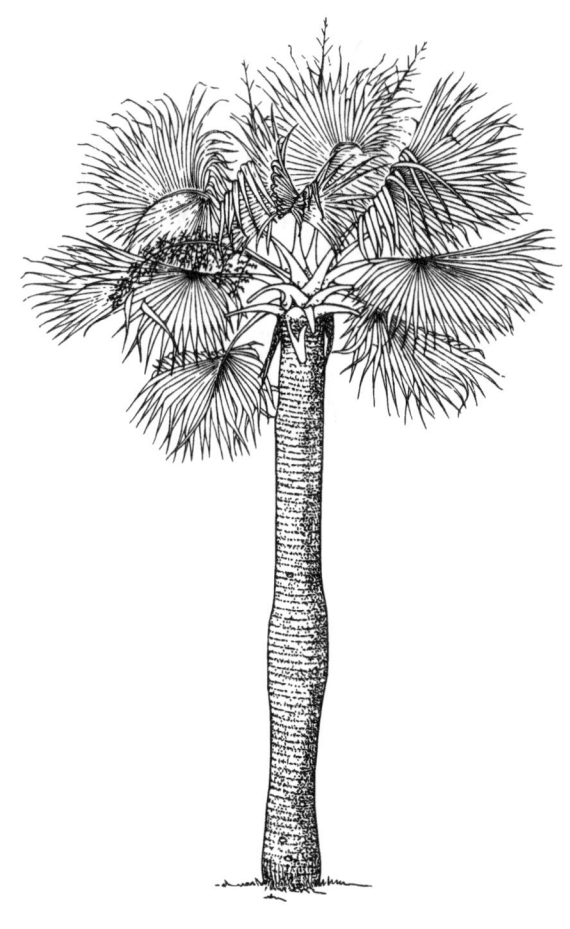

i could use a beach day...

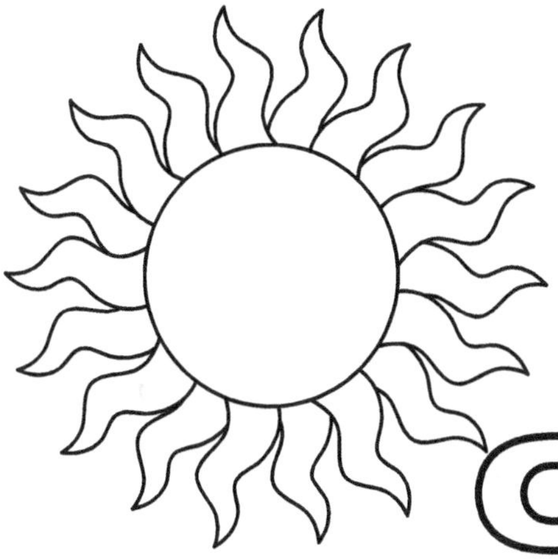

ON A BEACH SIPPIN' SOMETHING STRONG

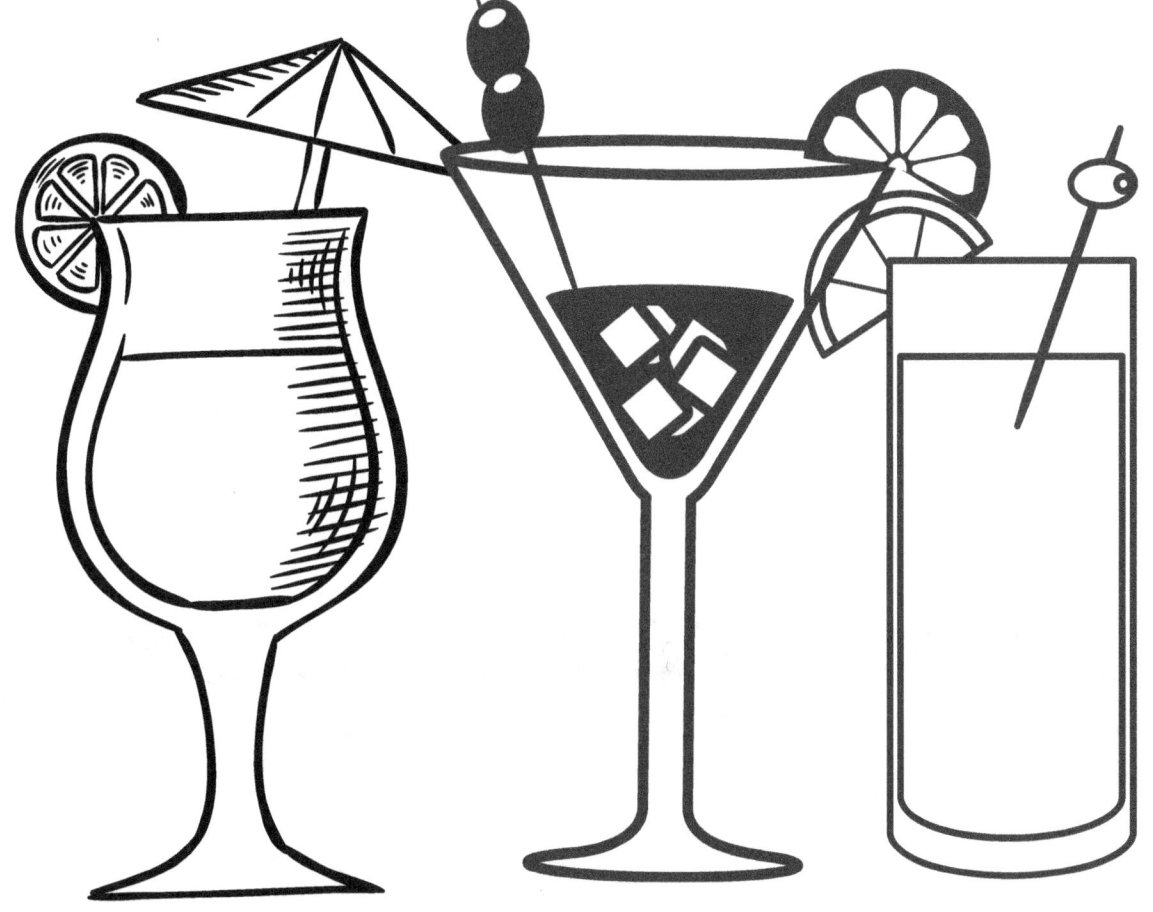

palms, palms, palms

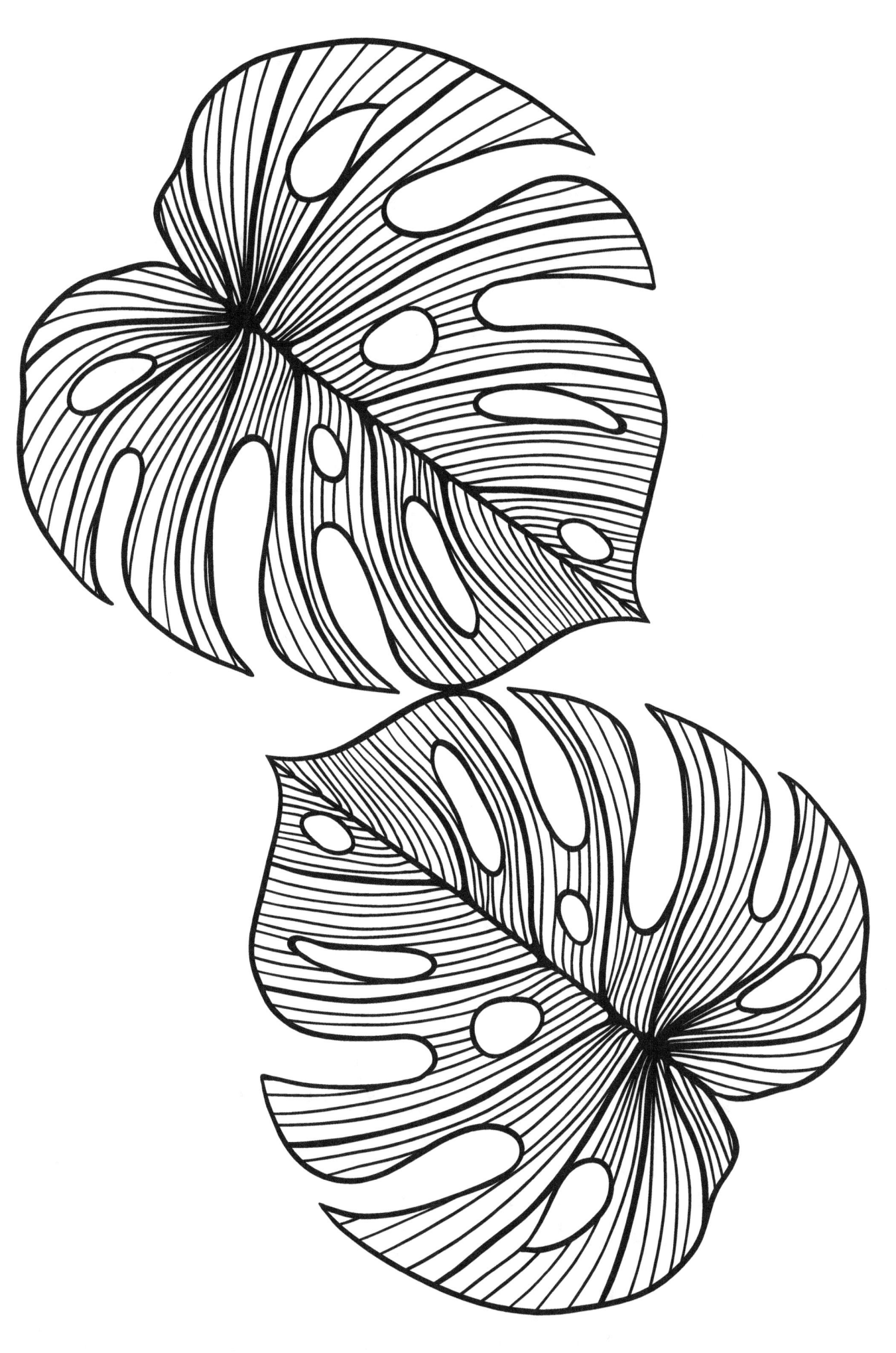

sunflowers by the beach

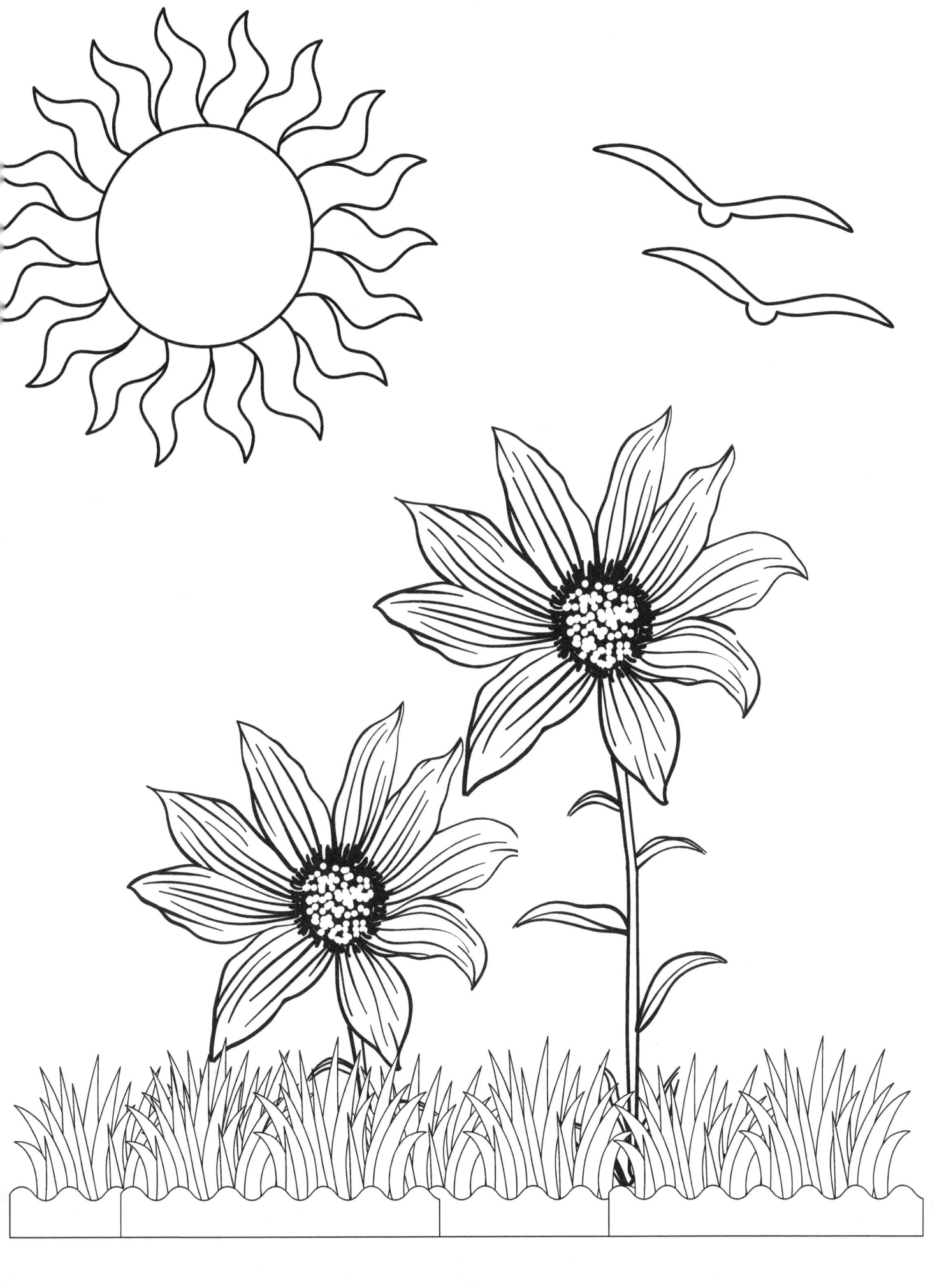

don't go coco-nuts

ABOUT TO GO COCO NUTS

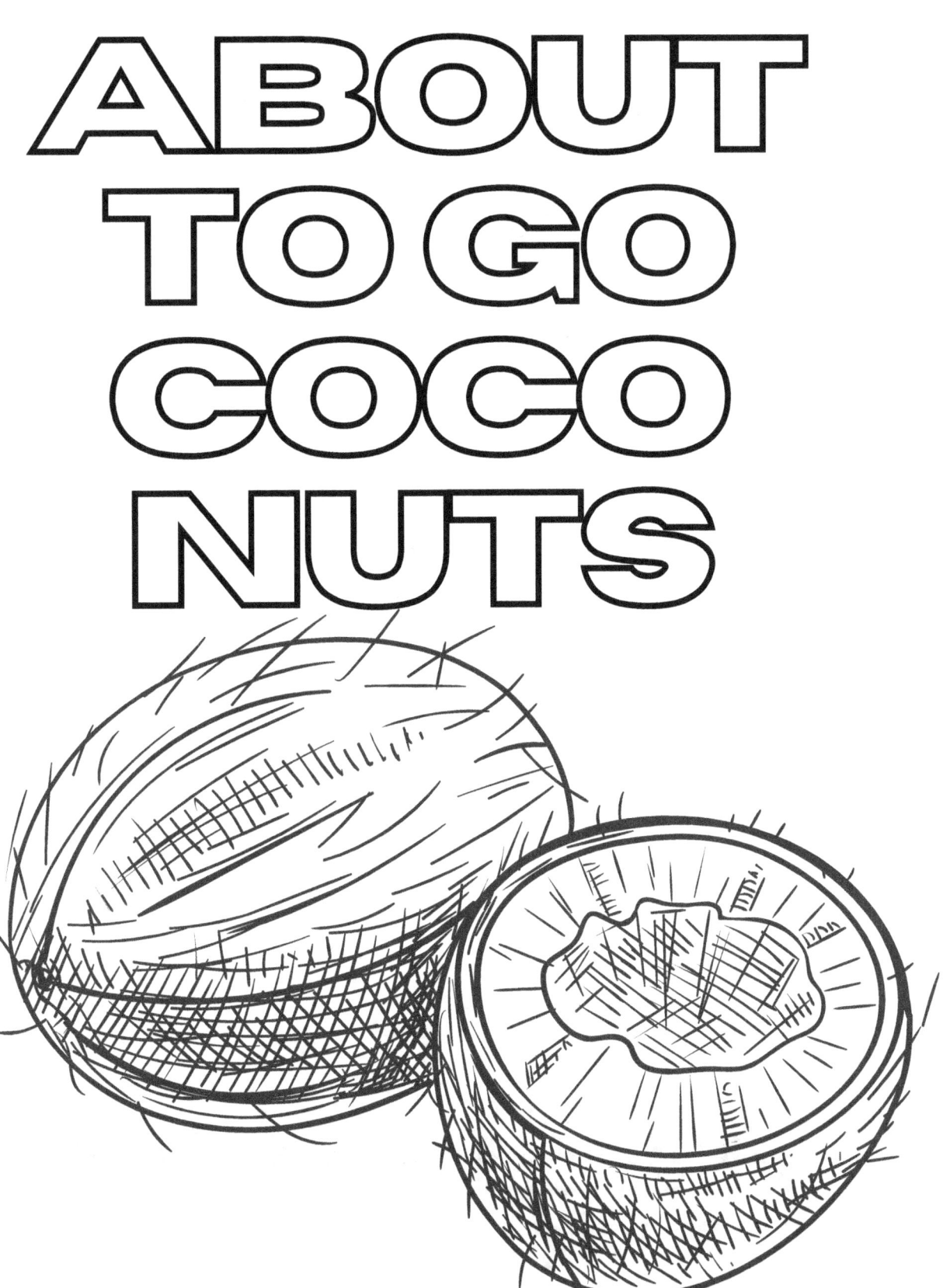

pineapples, pineapples, pineapples

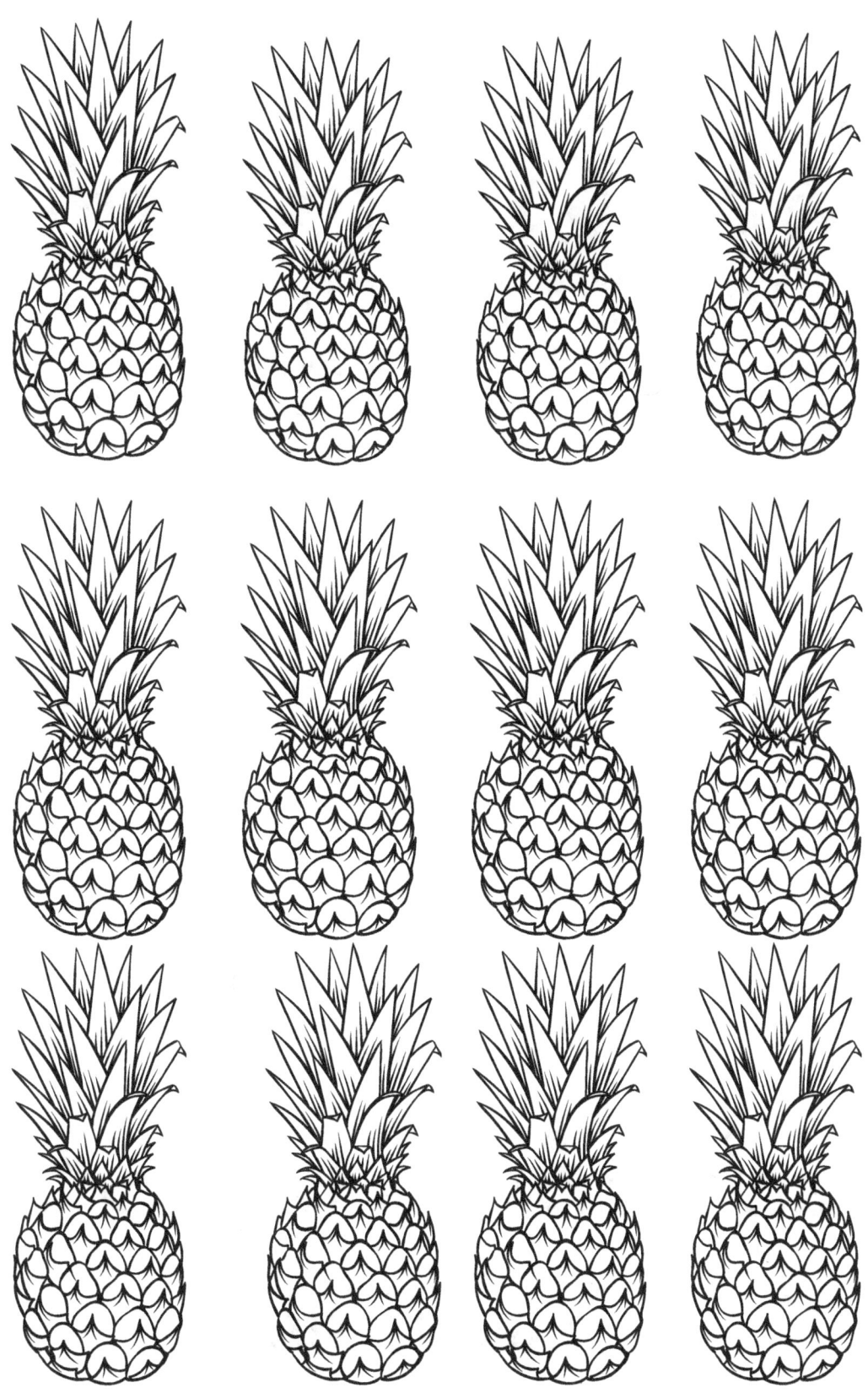

saltwater is the best
medicine

SALT WATER

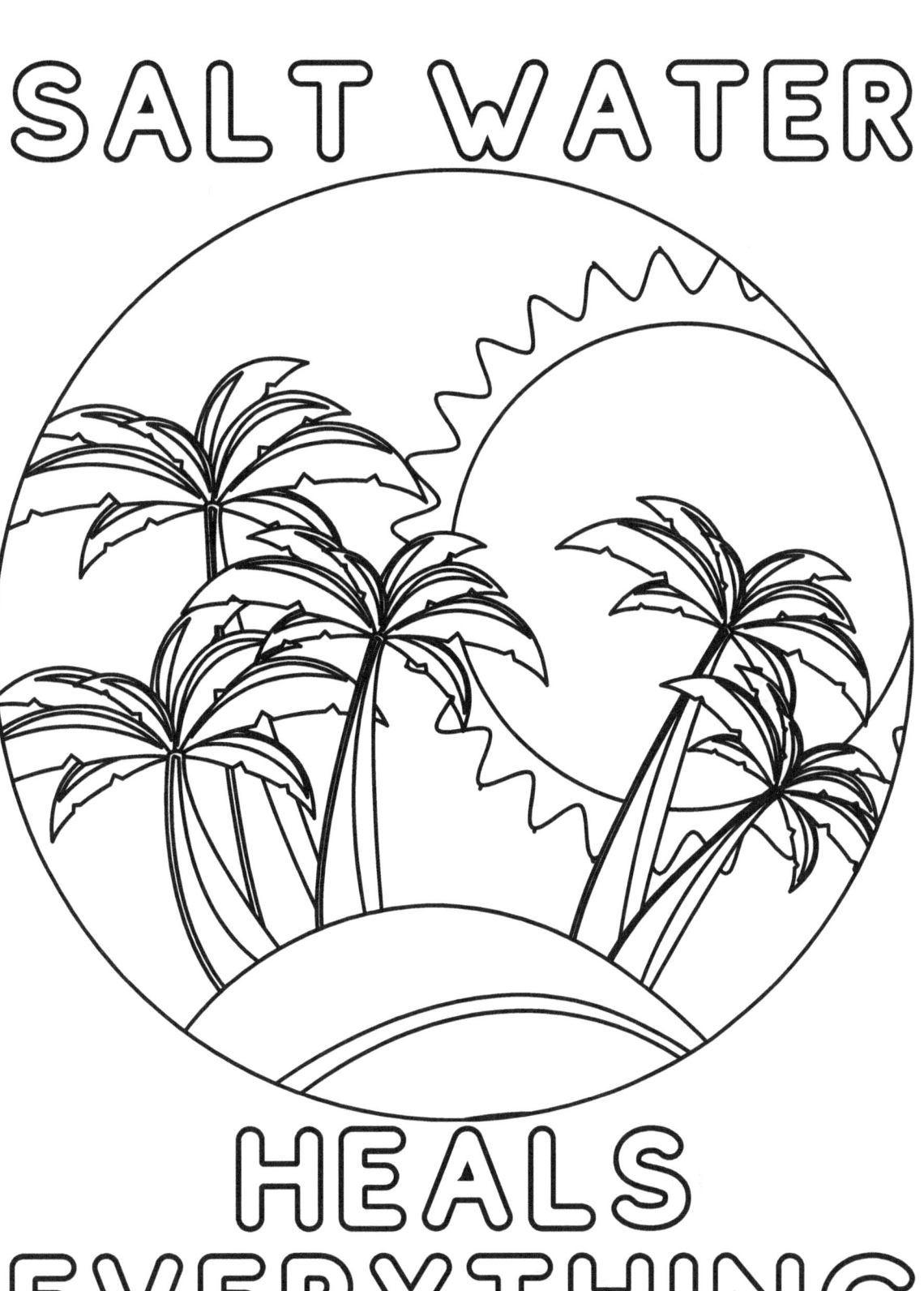

HEALS
EVERYTHING

tropical vibes are the
best vibes

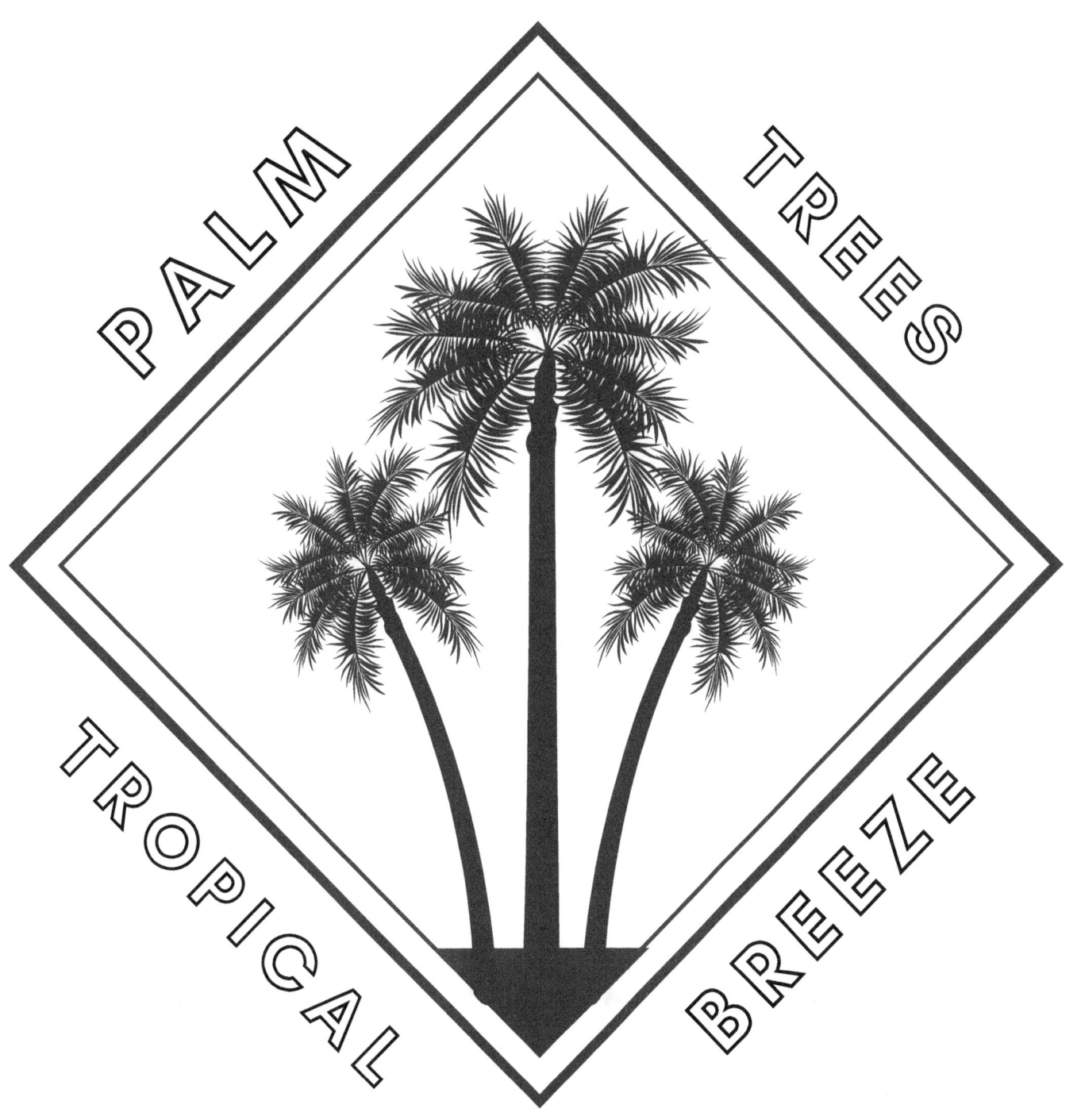

be a tropical plant mom for
vacation mode everyday

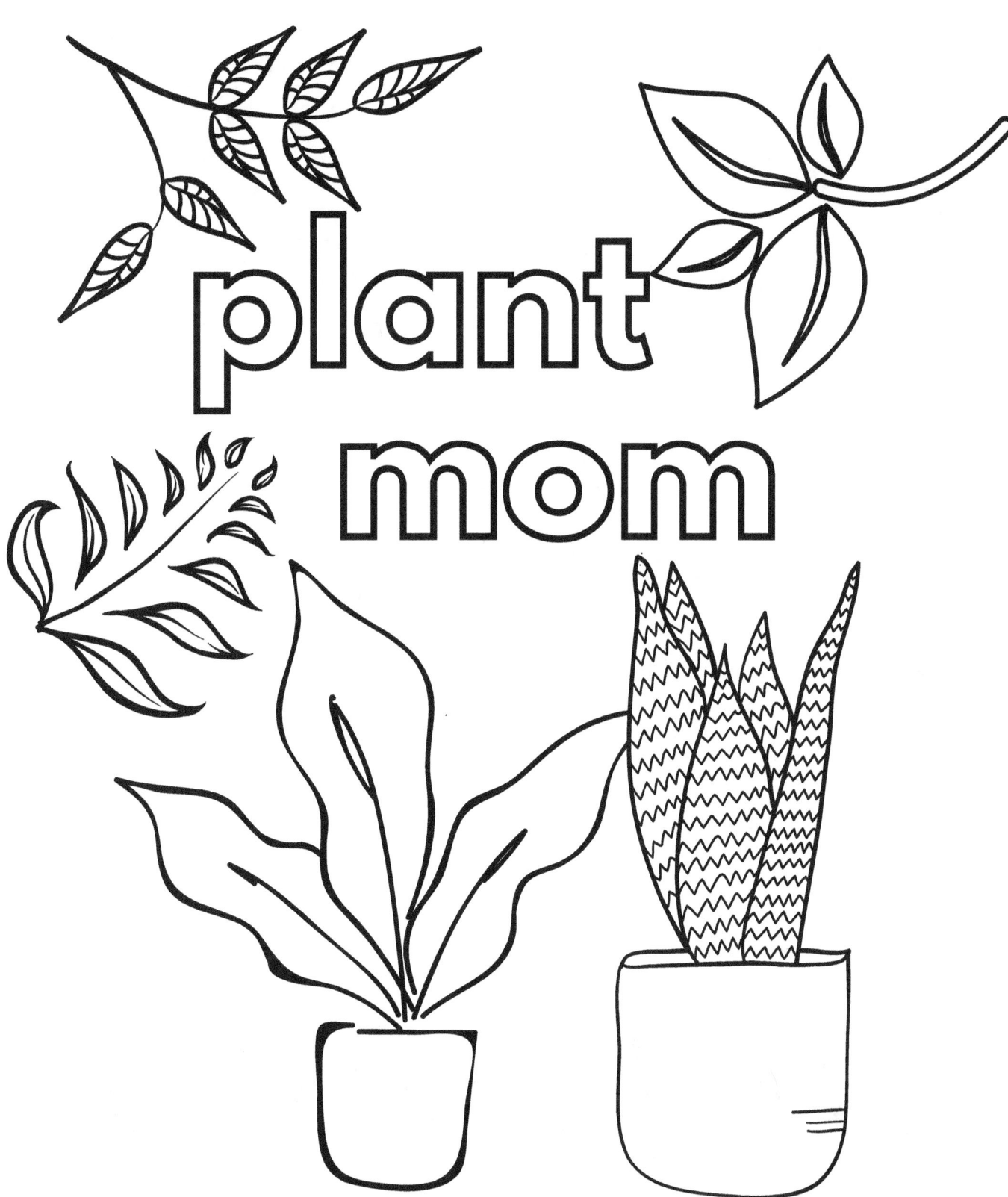

time to book a trip

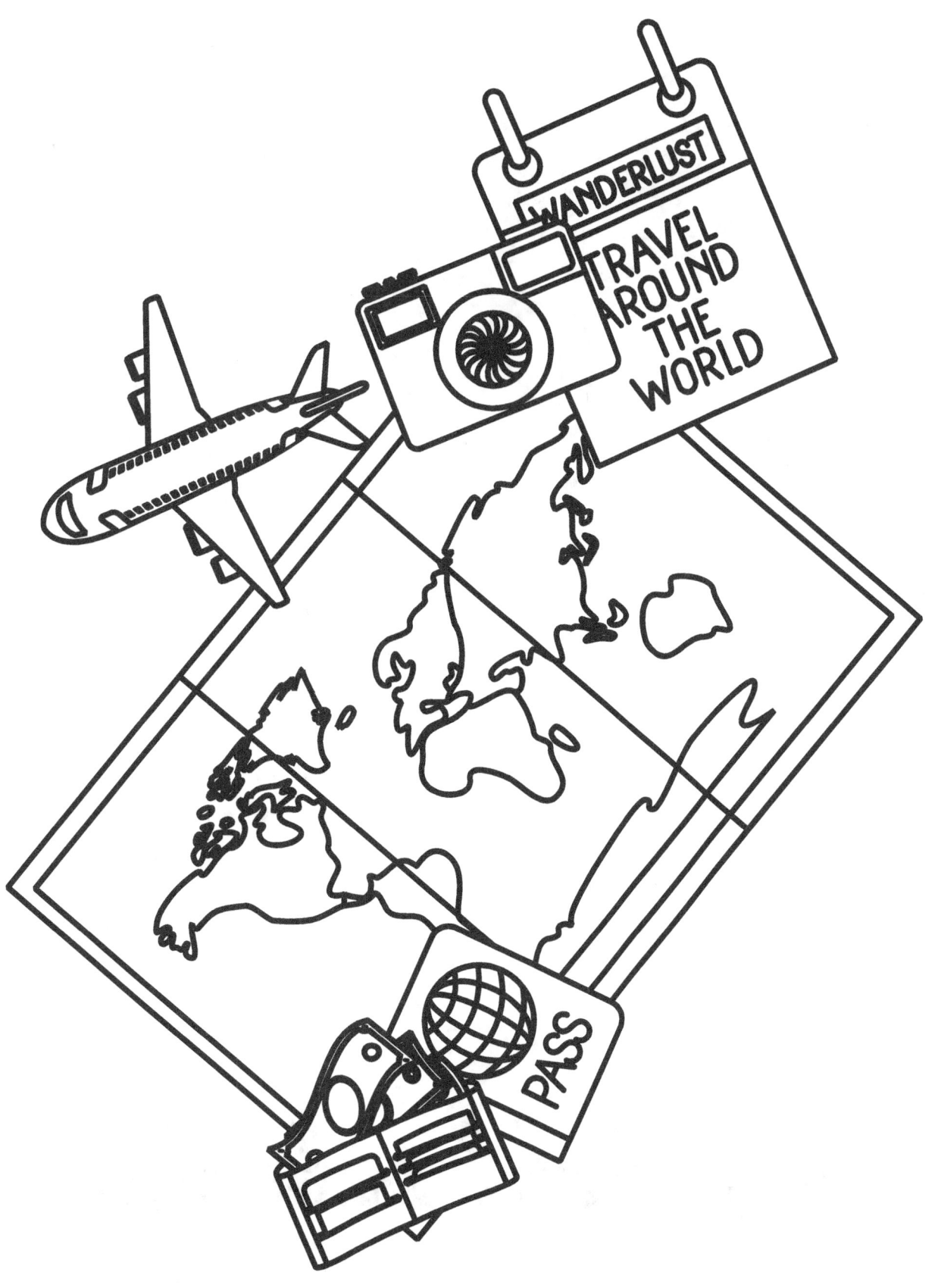

my flight is booked

LETS GET
AWAY

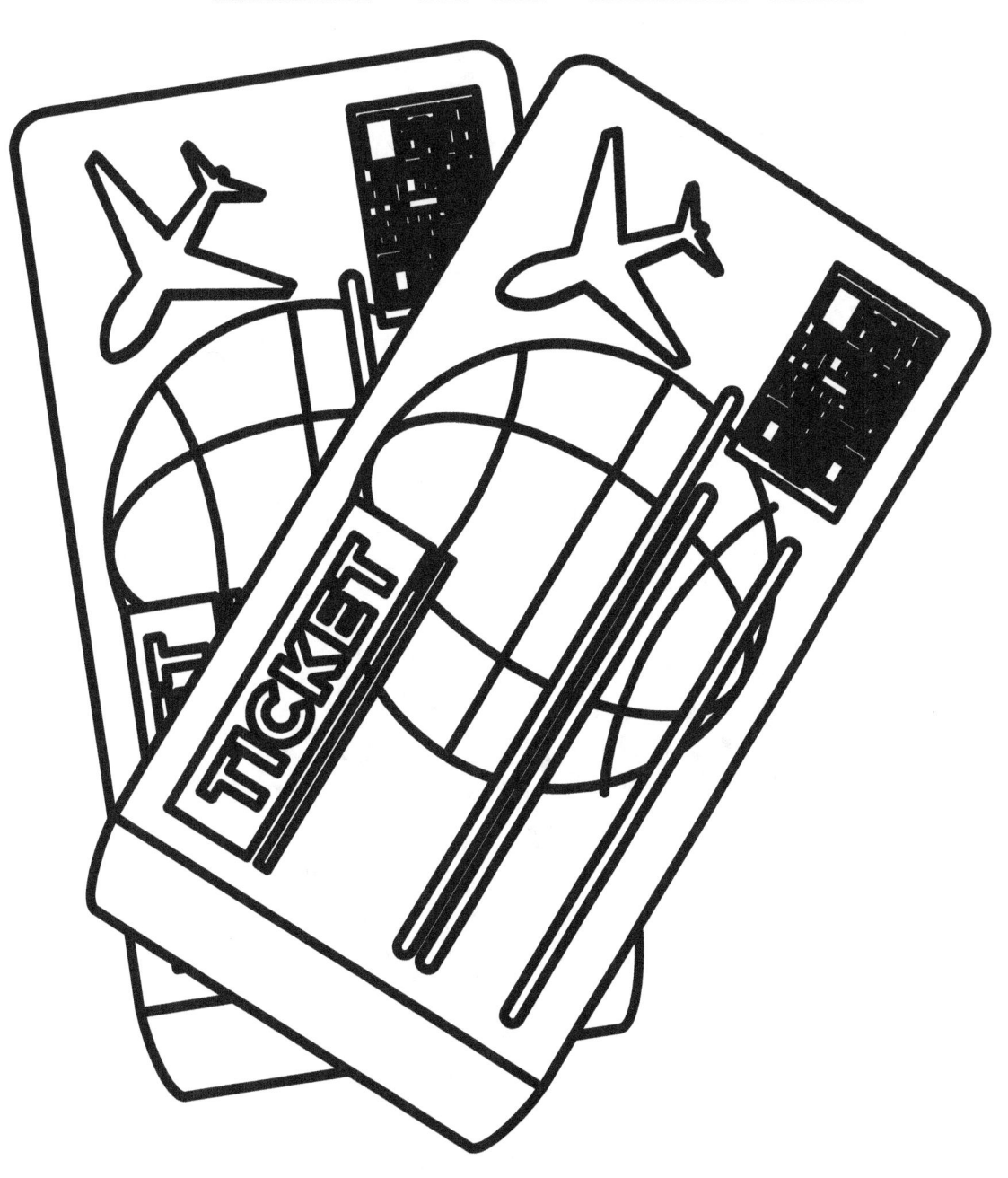

wishing I was
on a boat

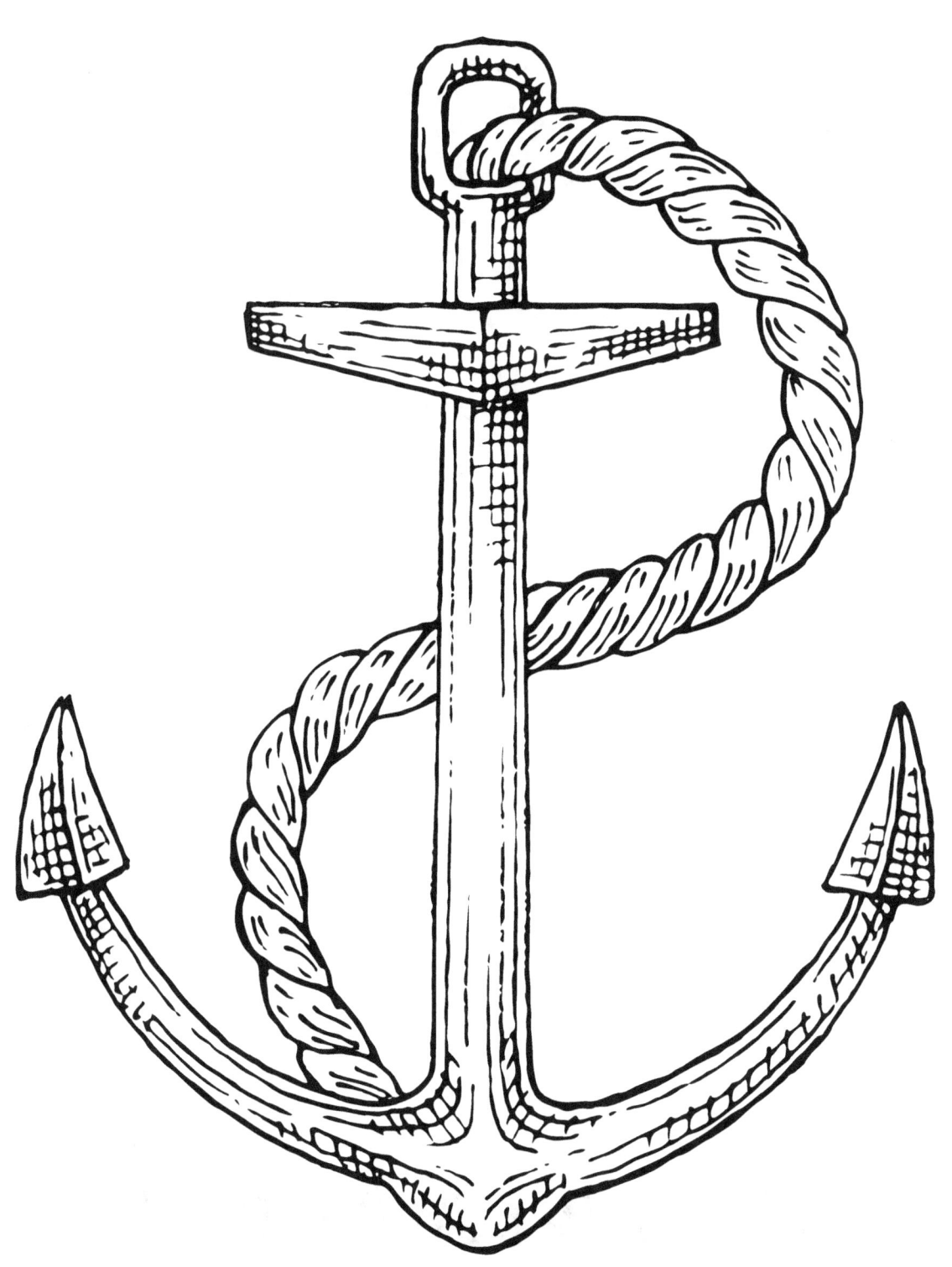

you're amazing!

REMEMBER YOU'RE A PEARL NOT A CLAM

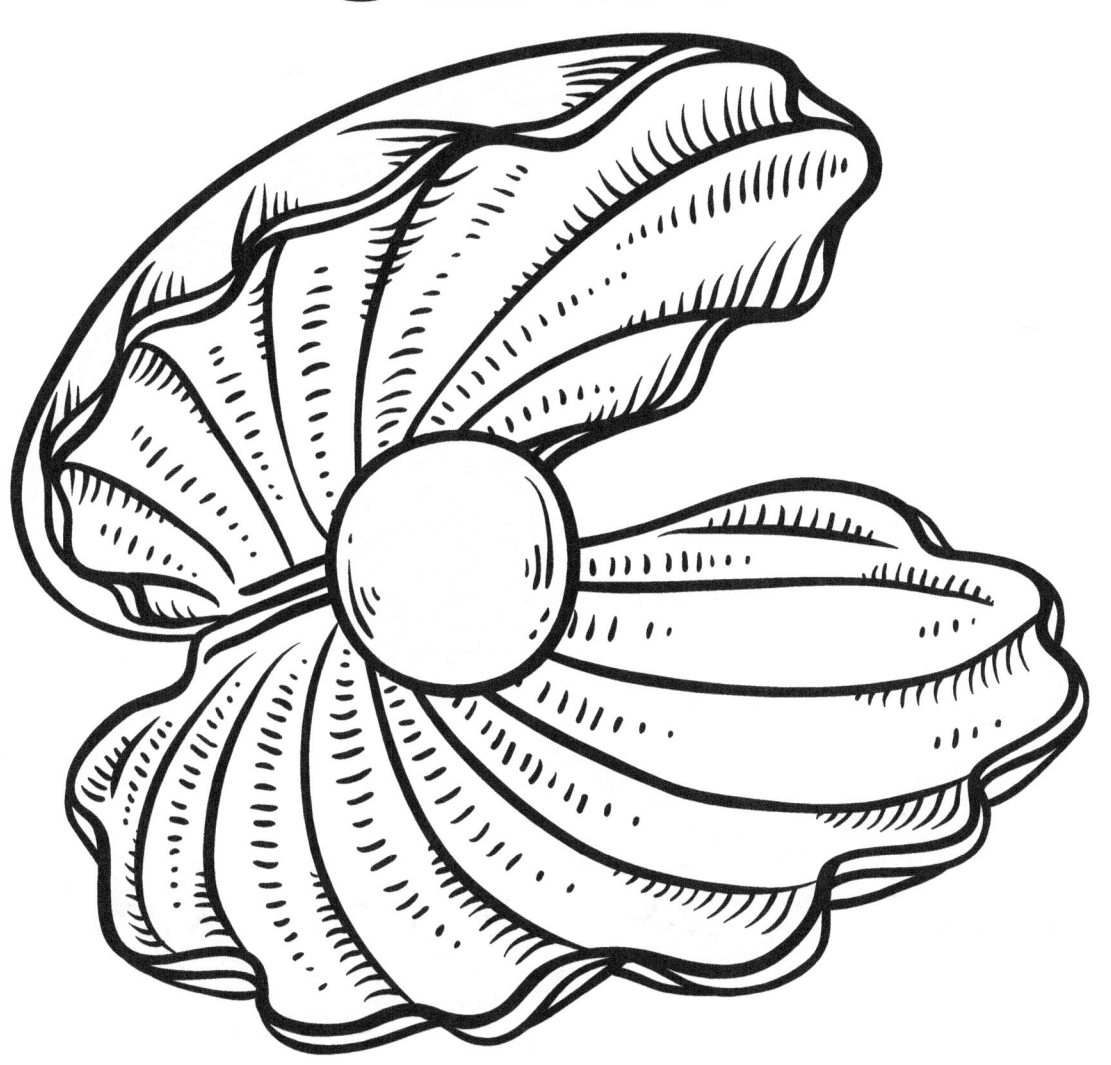

anchor anchor anchor

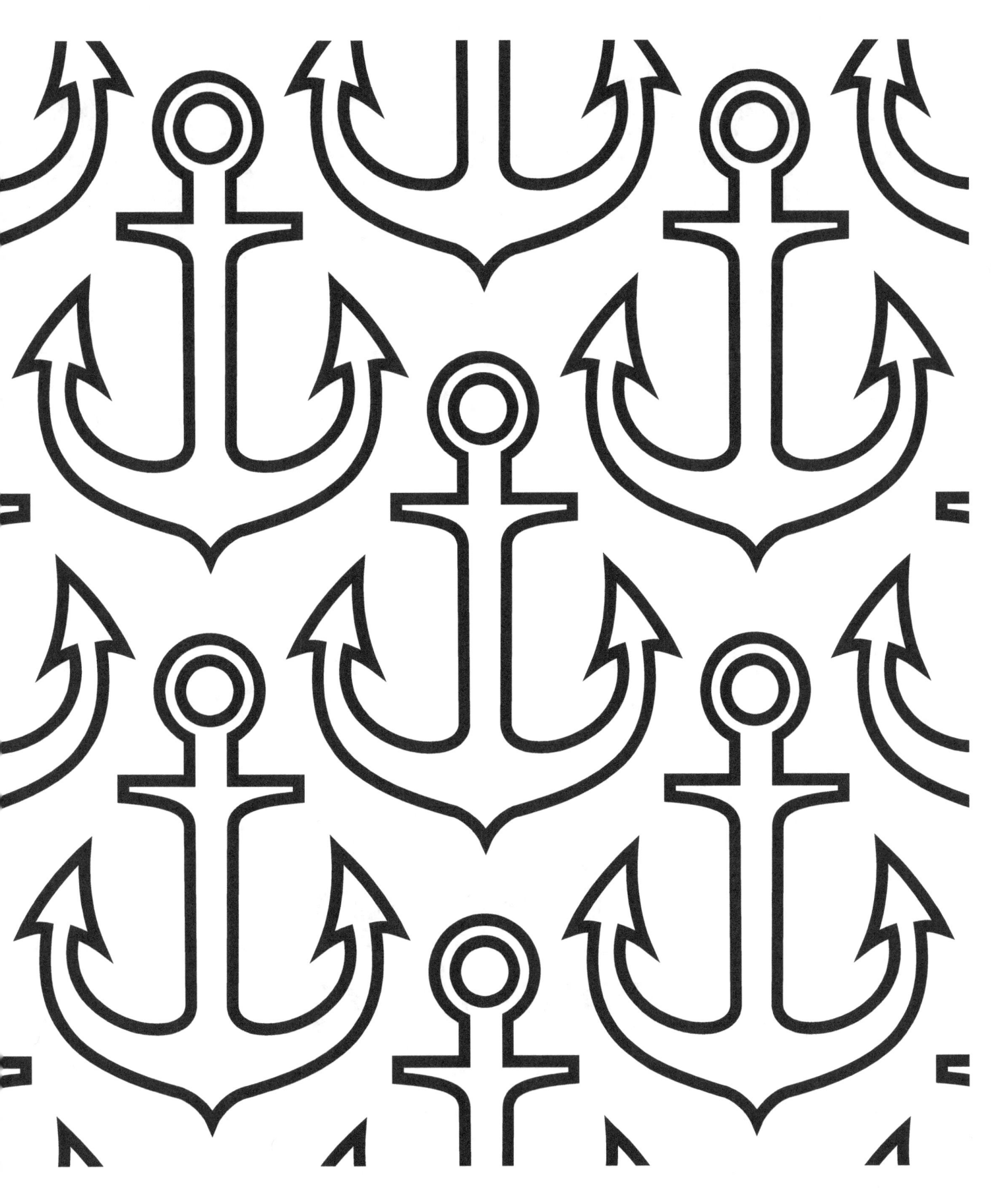

it's time for your
sunnies honey

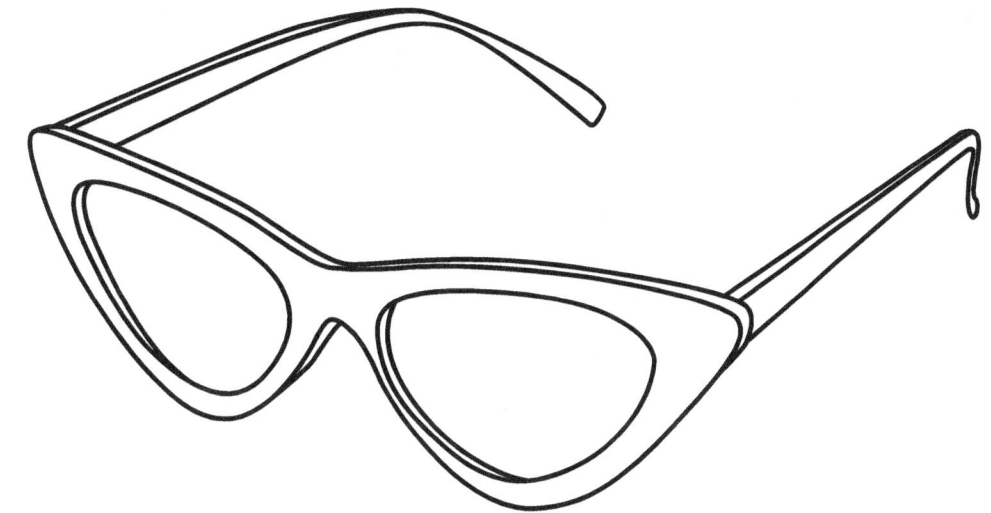

I'VE GOT MY
SUNNIES
HONEY

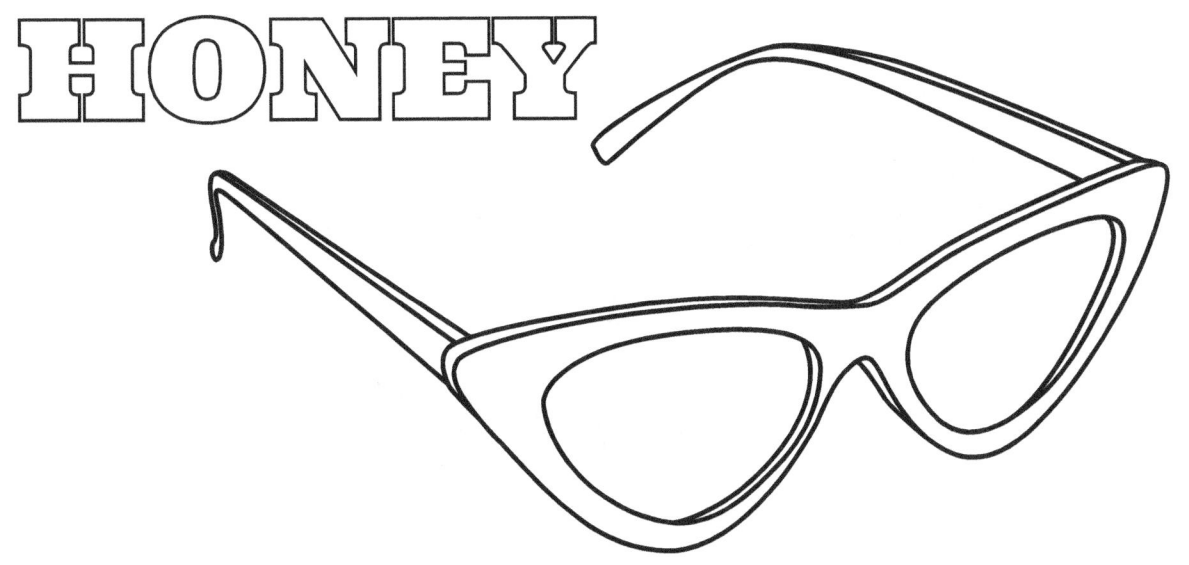

the only vitamin
I need

VITAMIN SEA

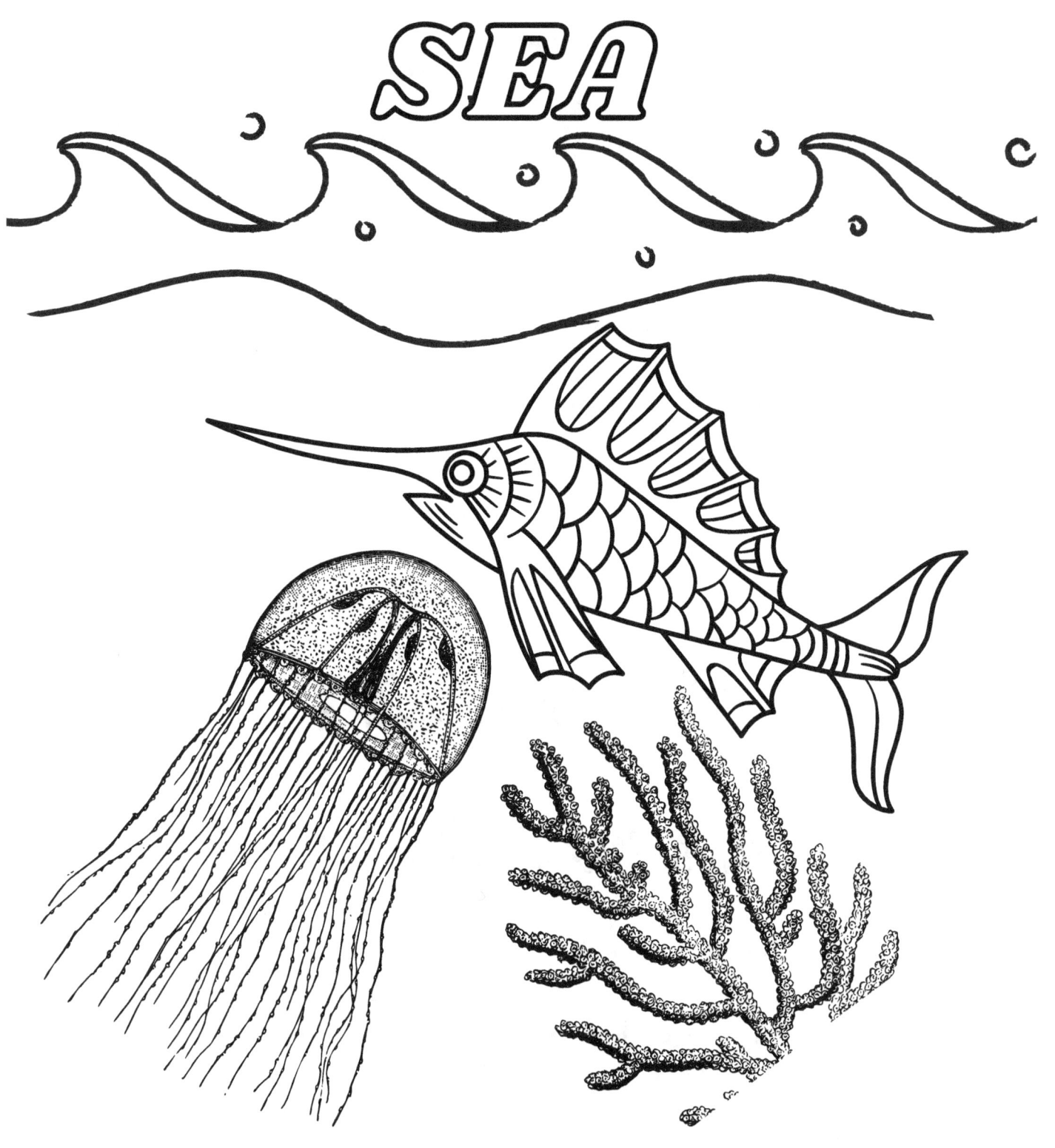

*never miss
an adventure*

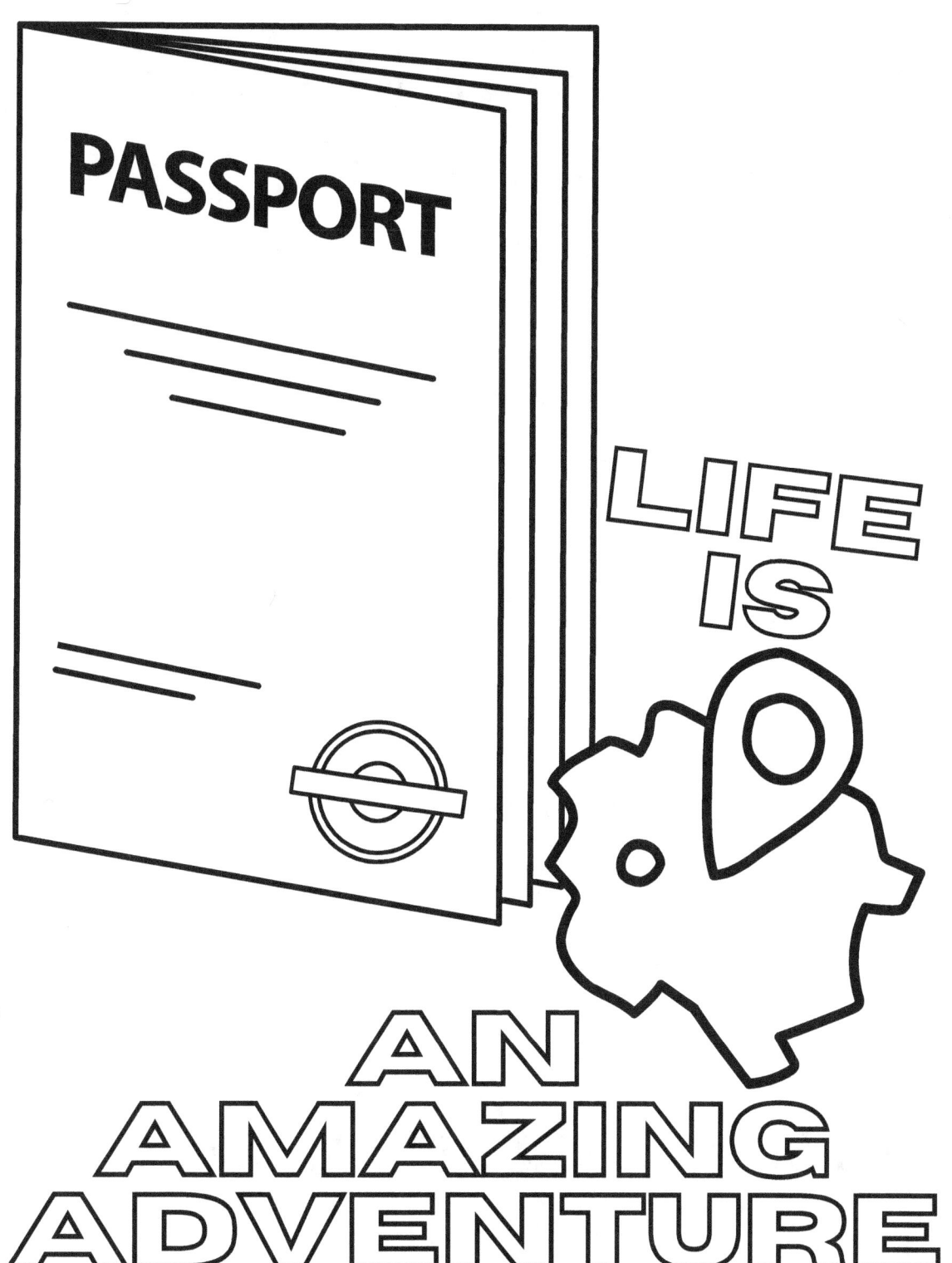

seahorse, seahorse, seahorse

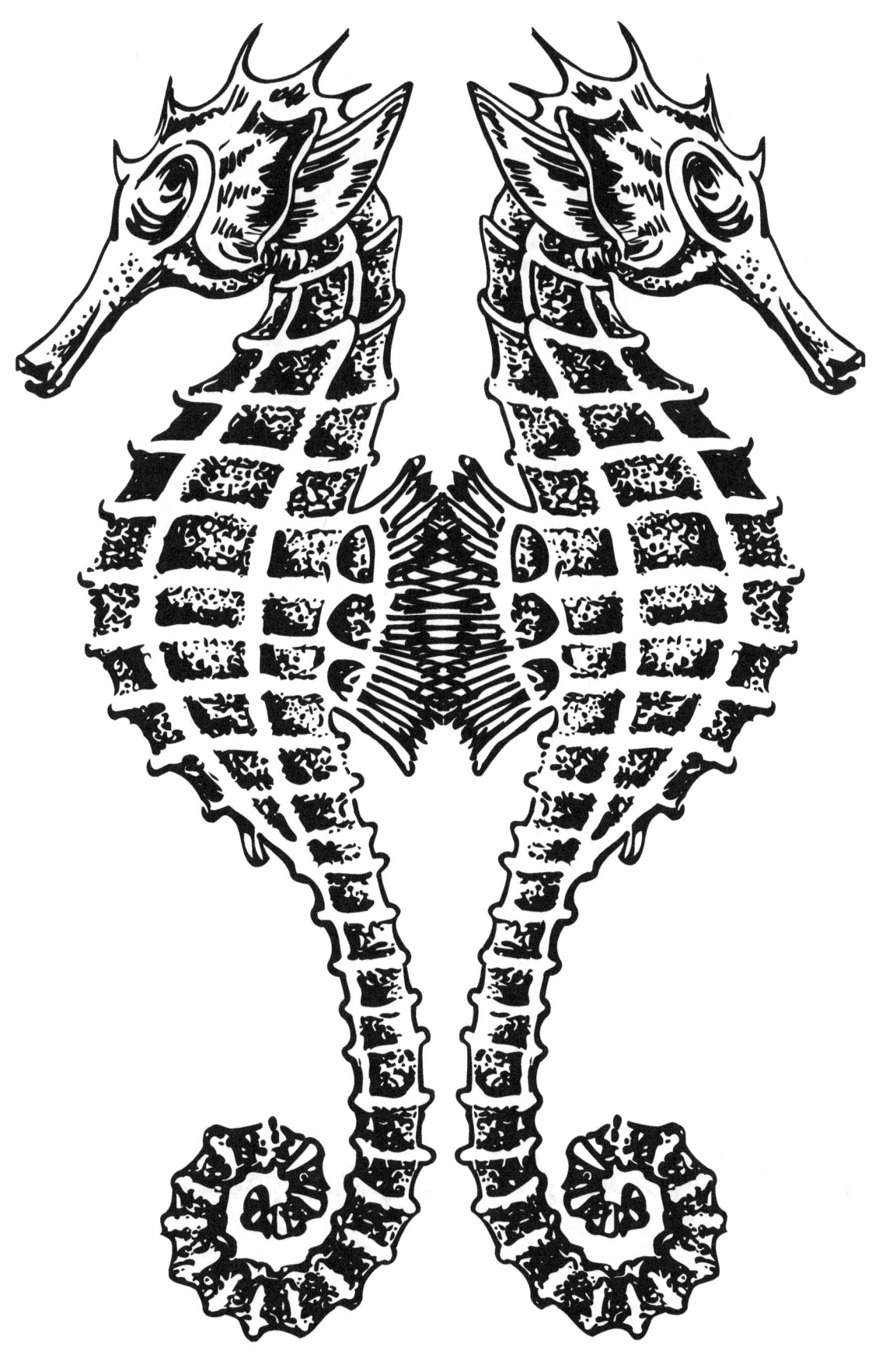

flamingos, flamingos, flamingos

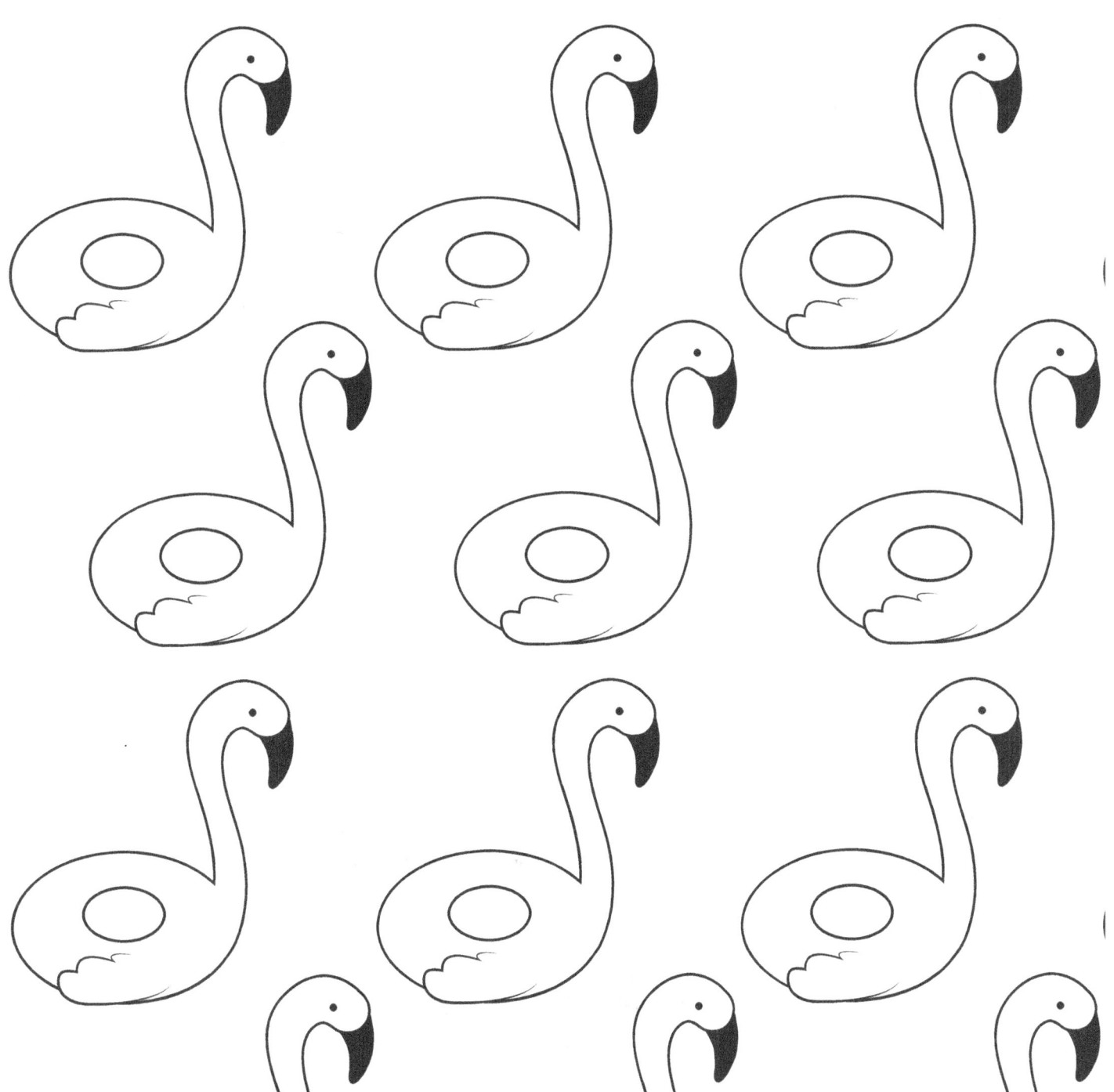

*I would love
a margarita*

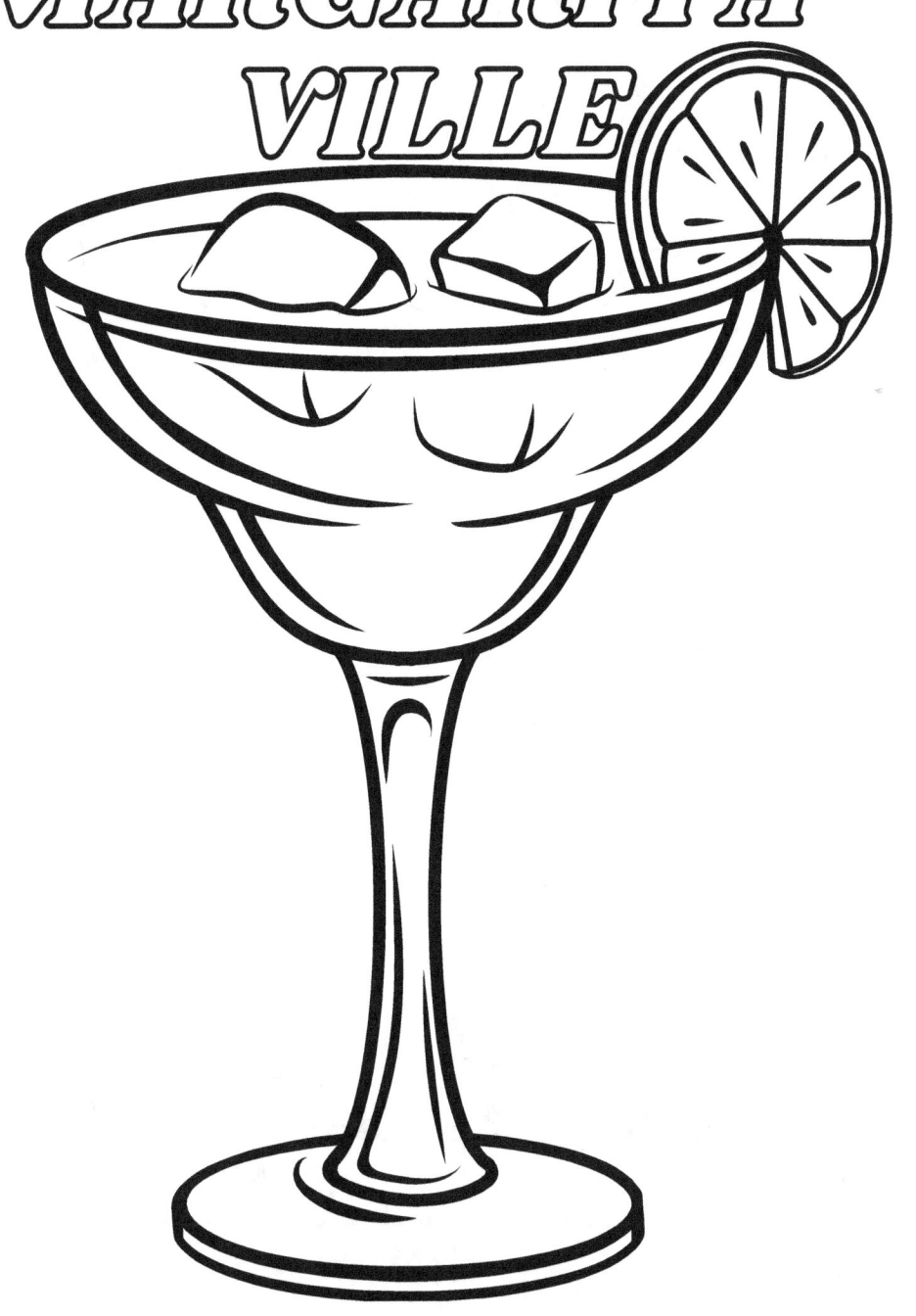

beach sipping

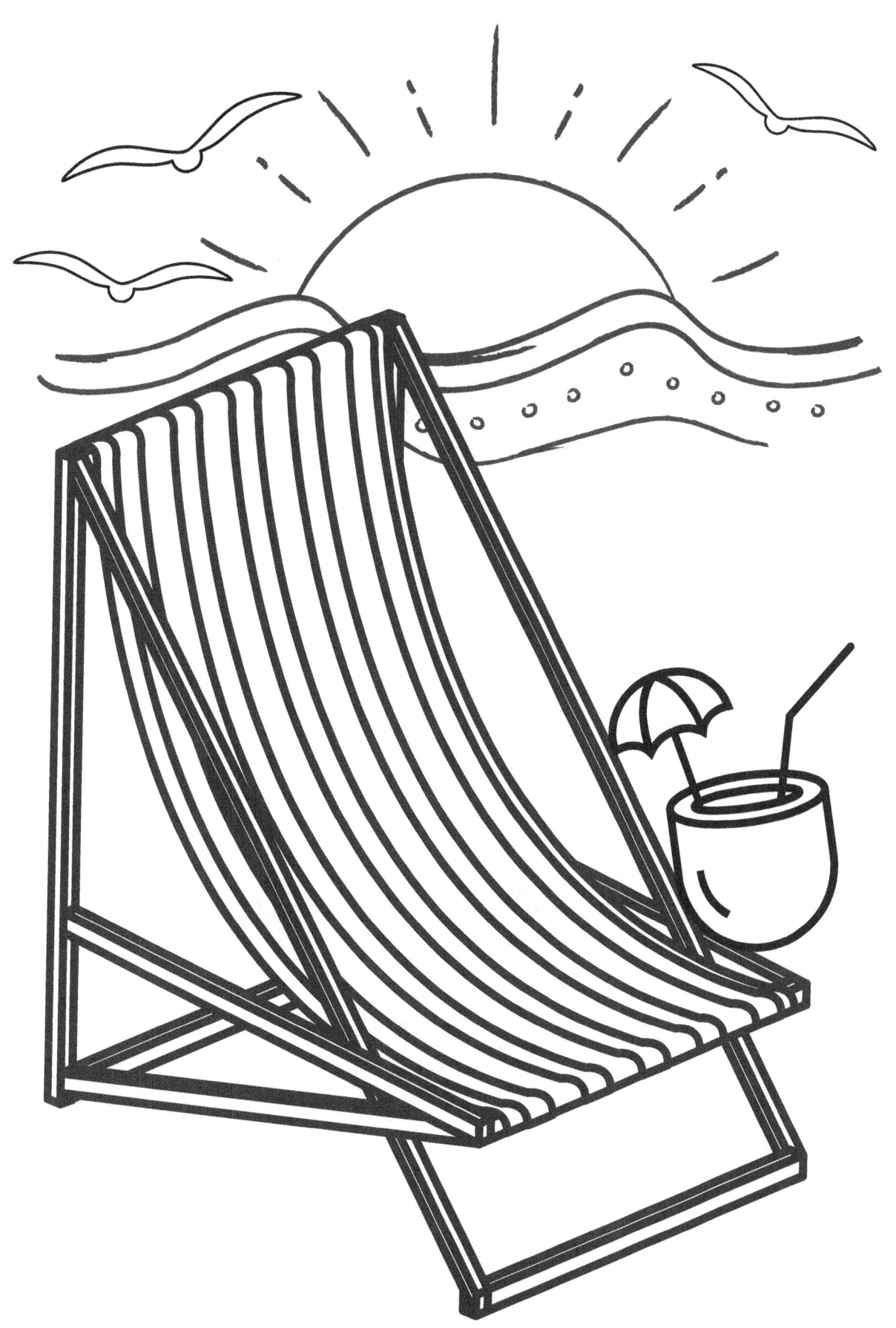

find some

shells

WHAT THE SHELL

love the ocean

I'M HAPPIEST

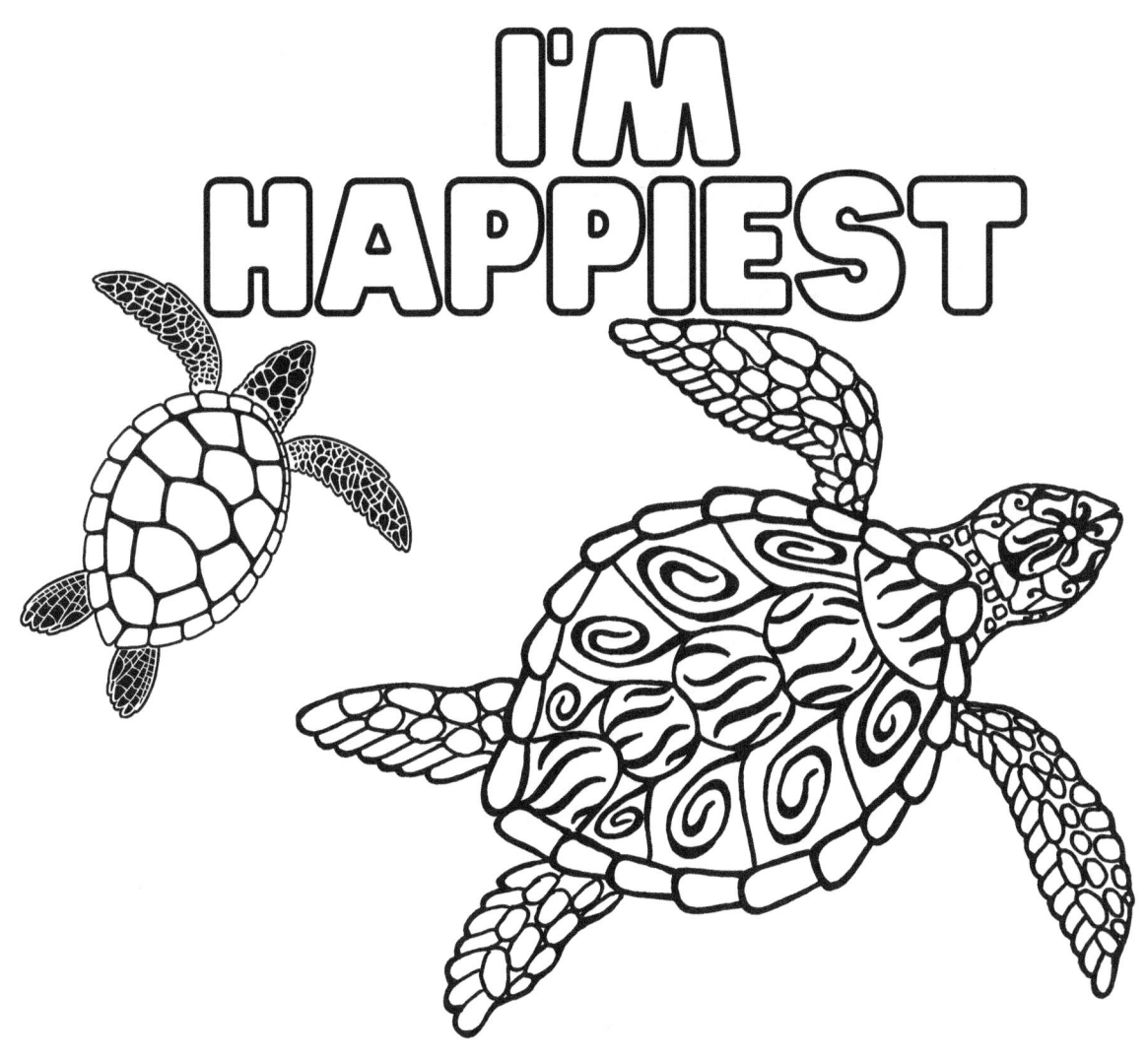

WHEN I'M FLOATING IN THE SEA